ROBERTO

Pride of the Pittsburgh Pirates

CLEMENTE

BY JONAH WINTER

ILLUSTRATED BY

RAÚL COLÓN

HAMPTON-BROWN

Can your
goals affect
other people? How?

Roberto Clemente wants to be a great baseball player.
He starts playing baseball as a boy with a stick and a can.
He becomes a major league player who
is very exciting to watch.

On an island called Puerto Rico,
where **baseball players are as plentiful**

as tropical flowers in a rain forest,
there was a boy who **had very little**

but **a fever** to play
and win at baseball.

....

baseball players are as plentiful there are as many baseball players
had very little was very poor
a fever who really wanted

He had no money for a baseball bat,
so he made one from a **guava** tree branch.

His first glove he also made,
from the cloth of a coffee-bean sack.

His first baseball field was muddy
and crowded with palm trees.

For batting practice he used empty soup cans
and hit them farther than anyone else.

Soup cans
turned into softballs.

Softballs
turned into baseballs.

Little League turned into
minor league turned into

winter league: professional baseball
in Puerto Rico. He played so well

....

guava fruit

he received an invitation
to play in . . . the major leagues

in America!
What an honor!

But the young man was sent to a **steel-mill town**
called Pittsburgh, Pennsylvania,

where his new team, the Pittsburgh Pirates,
was in *last place*.

Now this was something very strange,
being on a losing team.

For the young Puerto Rican,
everything was strange.

Instead of palm trees, he saw **smokestacks**.
Instead of Spanish, he heard English.

Instead of being *somebody*,
he was nobody.

....

steel-mill town town with a lot of factories
smokestacks tall chimneys rising above factories

BEFORE YOU MOVE ON...

1. **Conflict** Reread page 6. The story started with a problem. What was it?

2. **Comparisons** How was Pittsburgh, Pennsylvania different from Puerto Rico?

LOOK AHEAD Does Roberto help his new team? Read pages 7–13 to find out.

His first time at bat,
He heard the announcer **stumble through** his Spanish name:

"ROB, uh, ROE . . . BURRT,
um, let's see, TOE

CLUH-MAINT?"
It echoed in the **near-empty stands**.

Roberto Clemente was his name,
And this is pronounced "Roe-BEAR-toe Cleh-MEN-tay."

As if to introduce himself,
Roberto *smacked* the very first pitch.

....

stumble through have problems saying
near-empty stands ballpark seats that were almost empty
smacked hit

7

But it went right up the infield . . .
And into the second baseman's glove.

Still, Roberto ran like lightning—
and **beat the throw to first base**.

The Pittsburgh fans **checked** their scorecards.
Who was this guy, "Roberto Clemente"?

....

beat the throw to first base got to first base
checked looked at

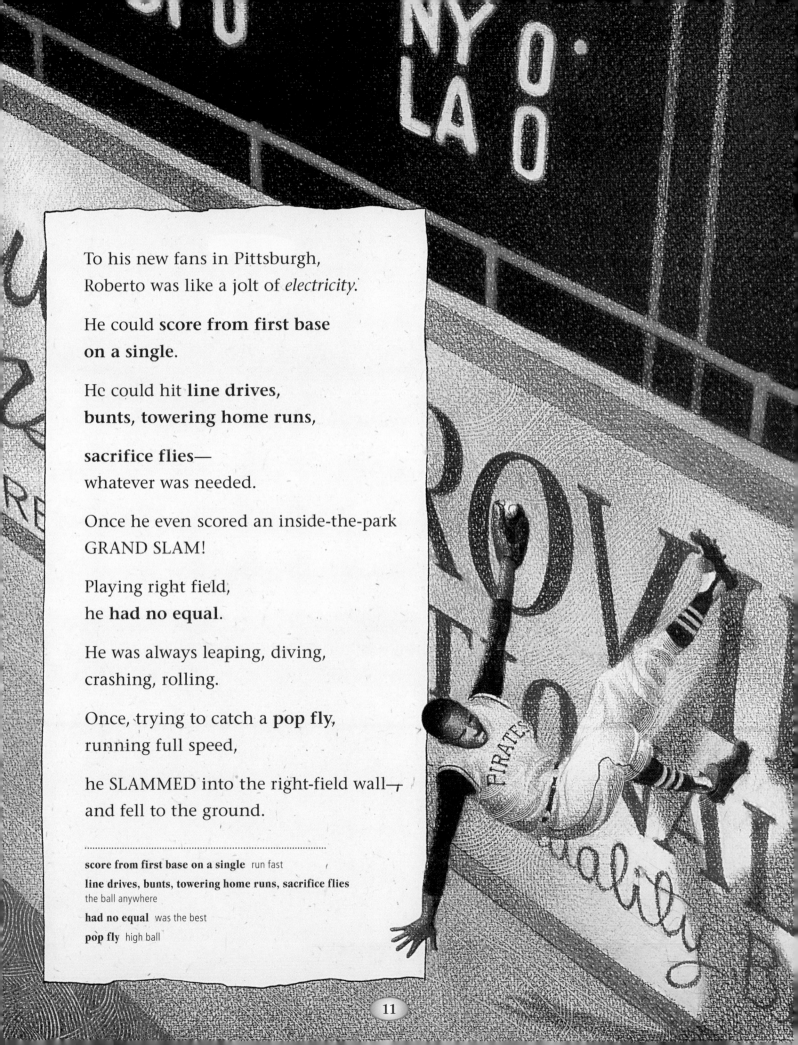

To his new fans in Pittsburgh,
Roberto was like a jolt of *electricity*.

He could **score from first base
on a single.**

He could hit **line drives,
bunts, towering home runs,**

sacrifice flies—
whatever was needed.

Once he even scored an inside-the-park
GRAND SLAM!

Playing right field,
he **had no equal.**

He was always leaping, diving,
crashing, rolling.

Once, trying to catch a **pop fly,**
running full speed,

he SLAMMED into the right-field wall—
and fell to the ground.

---

score from first base on a single run fast
line drives, bunts, towering home runs, sacrifice flies
the ball anywhere
had no equal was the best
pop fly high ball

At last, slowly, he lifted his glove.
The ball was inside.

....

At last Finally

BEFORE YOU MOVE ON...

1. **Inference** Roberto helped the Pittsburgh Pirates. What tells you that the fans in Pittsburgh liked him?

2. **Summarize** What was Roberto's experience playing for the team?

LOOK AHEAD Read pages 14–17 to find out what Roberto helps his team do next.

Roberto is a great baseball player. Kids want to be just like him. He works hard and helps give Pittsburgh fans a reason to celebrate.

But it wasn't just how he played.
He had *style*. **He was** *cool*.

He had this move he did with his neck
before each **at bat**,

creaking it one way,
then the other.

Soon kids who wanted to be just like Roberto
were doing it, too, twisting their necks this way and that.

Roberto did it to **ease** the pain he felt
from playing **his heart out** in every game.

"If you don't try as hard as you can," he said,
"you are wasting your life."

....

He had *style*. **He was** *cool*. He was interesting and exciting.
at bat time it was his turn to hit
creaking tilting, moving
ease help with
his heart out the hardest he could

Roberto tried so hard,
he helped the last-place Pirates

make it all the way to the World Series
where they beat the **mighty** NEW YORK YANKEES!

....

make it all the way to win so many games that they got to play in
mighty great

After the series,
down in the streets of Pittsburgh,

Roberto walked alone among his fans,
who were so busy celebrating,

....

down in on

they didn't even notice him.
That didn't bother Roberto.

He was happy to **feel lost in the crowd
of** a party he had helped create.

....

feel lost in the crowd of be celebrating alone at

BEFORE YOU MOVE ON...

1. **Conclusions** Roberto helped the Pirates win the World Series. During the celebration, none of his fans noticed him. Why didn't this bother him?

2. **Paraphrase** Reread page 14. What did Roberto mean when he said, "If you don't try as hard as you can, you are wasting your life"?

LOOK AHEAD Read pages 18–21 to find out what makes Roberto unhappy.

But there was something
that would have made **Roberto's joy a little sweeter**.

As much as fans loved him,
the newspaper writers did not.

When Roberto was in such pain he couldn't play,
they called him "lazy."

They **mocked** his Spanish accent,
and when Roberto got angry,

the mainly white newsmen
called him a Latino **"hothead."**

Roberto **swore** he would be so good,
he would *have* to get the respect he deserved.

He would become the greatest all-around baseball player
there ever was.

At home that Christmas,
Roberto went back to the same muddy field

he'd played on as a boy.
In his pocket was a bag full of bottle caps

that he emptied into the hands of some kids.
They threw him the caps, and he hit each one

again
and again.

....

Roberto's joy a little sweeter Roberto even happier
mocked made fun of
"hothead" angry man
swore promised himself

When he returned to Pittsburgh **come** spring,
baseballs looked HUGE,

and he **clobbered them as never before**.
That season, he hit .351,

the highest batting average
in the National League.

....

come in the

clobbered them as never before hit them harder than he ever
had before

BEFORE YOU MOVE ON...

1. **Inference** Roberto was unhappy because the newspaper writers criticized him. Why did this bother Roberto?

2. **Cause and Effect** What did Roberto do in Puerto Rico that helped him when he got back to Pittsburgh?

LOOK AHEAD Read pages 22–25 to find out what Roberto proves to the world.

Roberto really wants respect. He plays so well that he begins to get it. He uses his fame to help those who are in need.

And still he did not get the **credit**
he deserved for being so great.

"It's because I'm black, isn't it?"
he asked the sneering reporters.

"It's because I am Puerto Rican.
It's because I am proud."

It was starting to seem
as if Roberto might never be respected

in the big world outside of Pittsburgh
and Puerto Rico. And then something happened.

The year was 1971.
The Pirates were in the World Series again,

playing against the Baltimore Orioles,
who **were favored** to win.

All around America and Puerto Rico,
people sat watching on TV . . .

As Roberto **put on a one-man show.**
Stealing bases, hitting home runs,

....

credit praise, honor

were favored everyone thought were going

put on a one-man show played harder than anyone else in the
game

22

playing right field with **a *fire***
most fans had never seen before.

Finally, *finally,*
it could not be **denied**:

---

a *fire* passion
denied argued

Roberto was the greatest all-around baseball player of his time, maybe of all time.

BEFORE YOU MOVE ON...

1. **Main Idea and Details** Roberto proved that he was the best all-around baseball player of his time. How?

2. **Conclusions** Roberto thought that he did not get respect because he was Puerto Rican. Why did he think that?

LOOK AHEAD Read pages 26–32 to find out what other things Roberto does in his life.

The very next year, he did something
that few have ever done:

During the last game of the season,
Roberto walked to the plate,

creaked his neck, dug **in his stance**,
stuck his chin toward the pitcher,

and **walloped** a line drive
off the center-field wall—his *three thousandth* hit!

The crowd cheered, and they wouldn't stop cheering.
For many minutes the players stopped playing

and Roberto stood on second base, amazed.
How far he had come.

---

in his stance his foot into the dirt
walloped hit
How far he had come. He had achieved so much.

Roberto is now one of 11 players in major league history to get 3000 or more hits!

27

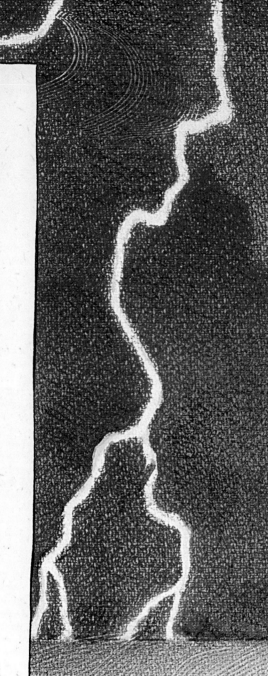

And yet, when the season was over,
the hero returned to the place where his story began,

to the land of muddy fields
and soup cans and bottle caps,

to his homeland of Puerto Rico,
where he was worshipped.

But did he sit around
and **polish his trophies**?

No. That rainy New Year's Eve,
Roberto sat in the San Juan airport

and waited for mechanics to fix the tired old airplane
that would take him to Central America.

There had been a terrible earthquake,
and he wanted to help the victims.

The plane would carry food and supplies
that Roberto had paid for.

Right before midnight, he **boarded**.
The rain was really **coming down**.

One of the propellers buzzed loudly.
As the plane took off,

the engines failed
and the plane fell into the ocean.

....

And yet Even though he was famous
polish his trophies think about how great he was
boarded got on the airplane
coming down bad

Just like that, it was over.
Roberto **was gone**.

How could his story
end this way,

so suddenly,
and with such sadness?

The story doesn't end here.
When someone like Roberto dies,

his **spirit** lives on
in the hearts of all he touched.

And Roberto's spirit is still growing.
It grows in the bats and gloves

and arms and legs of all the Latino baseball players
who have **flooded into** the major leagues.

His spirit grows in the charities he started
for poor people in Puerto Rico.

....

was gone had died
spirit memory
flooded into started playing in

And his spirit is still growing in Pittsburgh,
where people who saw him play

tell their children and grandchildren
of how he used to sparkle—running, diving,

firing game-saving throws
from deep right field

all the way to home plate—
SMACK—right into the catcher's glove.

....

of how he used to sparkle what a fantastic
baseball player he was

BEFORE YOU MOVE ON...

1. **Main Idea and Details** How did Roberto use his fame
   to help others?

2. **Paraphrase** Reread page 30. What did the author mean
   when he said that Roberto's "spirit lives on in the hearts
   of all he touched"?